To my husband:
Thank you for believing in my work and shining light in my dark tunnels when I couldn't seem to find my way out. I'm grateful for your continued reminder that I could follow my dreams and see them through.

I love you. ALWAYS!

Contents Page

Acknowledgments

To my parents: You all did the very best you could and knew how to. It is my privilege to watch you grow, shift, and change as I am doing. Thank you for your sacrifices and labors of love.

To my friends and siblings: Thank you for hyping me up and letting me know that my words have value. Thank y'all for holding me accountable, for asking me how things were coming along and listening to my heart when I felt entirely unsure of myself. I'm grateful for you all.

To my readers: Thank you for choosing this book. May you find something that resonates with your heart and soul. Cheers to being on the journey of being you!

Introduction

I started writing poetry and short stories around the age of seven. Writing was my refuge as I didn't feel I had an outlet for the BIG emotions that my body was carrying. Those emotions needed an escape route, so I created one. Writing was and still is a solace for me. It's a place of reflection, where I can deep dive and sort things out; it's a cleanse for me most of the time. It's a place where I navigate hard moments in my life. Writing was the place where I could be my most authentic self and no one would judge me for it.

My poetry was solely mine for a long time—then I met my husband, and he's been my sounding board ever since. He's usually the first to listen to my heart after my hands make the words clearer.

It has been a lifelong dream to have my poems published. Now that I'm here, present in my thirties, I've grappled with creating a book. What would people think? How would it be received? If there was a 'what' or 'how', I probably asked myself the question. As Brene Brown calls them, 'the shame gremlins' had taken hold of my mind for quite some time. The perfectionist in me wanted EVERYTHING to be right. Not a misspelled word, not a poem or word that would send me spiraling down the 'I'm not good enough for this' mindset. And if I'm honest with you, readers, I had to work my way through that similar process, prior to any of this ever being visible in the world.

This poetry book is a manifestation of my growth and joy, the releasing of my pain and sorrows. And although it isn't a full representation of my life, it was the sounding board to some of my loudest thoughts that, many times, I just couldn't shake until, like I mentioned before, I let the BIG emotions out. I had to write about them because I was having a hard time mentally navigating all my emotions in real time. May some of my words find you in your most necessary spaces.

Reflective Reminder:

1. You can do BIG things, even when they're HARD! (Especially when they're hard.)
2. Life is full of beautiful experiences easily shared with others, but hard moments should be shared too! (Specifically with people you trust.)
3. You are WORTHY! You ALWAYS have been, and ALWAYS will be.

Be brave with who you are. Be the most AUTHENTIC you, even when the task is daunting.

... Give You Something To Cry About

A Letter To My Father

Hey,

Twenty-two years ago, I was the product of your love for my mother. A decision was made that most parents couldn't dream of. I was given to a woman who would love and take care of me. I don't know when but, when the time came, the chance would magically appear. Who would've thought I'd be the smoke to the fire of my burning curiosity? Twenty-two years later, I have a visual, a voice, a slight sign of who I could've been, where I come from, and whom I resemble.

What I'm trying to say here is that regardless of what happened in the past, we only have *right now* to know each other. To talk to one another. To learn and grow a relationship with one another. I'm the woman I am today because of the decisions that were made twenty-two years ago, and I'll be forever grateful for them.

I know if you are anything like my mother, you have some regrets, some feelings that may make you shy away from having a relationship with me. Please understand, more than anything, the situation that was at hand, and I wouldn't ever be able to fully express the gratitude I have for the people and the experiences I've had because of the emotionally draining decisions that were made.

Look… I'm not asking for the world, I'm just asking you to be a part of it if you choose to. As my favorite quote says, "We don't try, we just do." So we can't just try to build a relationship, we have to just start building it.

I hope, for you, this letter brings clarity to how your daughter is and the way she thinks. Hopefully it sets your mind at ease and provides you with a sense of peace to move forward. I love you, and I hope that the upcoming year and the rest of this year will be the start to having a good and lasting relationship.

Little Girl

Inspired by the Jason Mraz song "Love is still the answer" (please listen to the live version on Youtube before reading)

For the sake of transparency, I have many parental units.

My adoptive mother, though a beautiful person, loved me so much that she became absent. Not absent as in I didn't see her, or feel her love, but absent in trying to figure her own shit out, in trying to ensure we had food on the table and clothes on our backs. She is strong, but she was absent for the cause. She left me in the good hands of my grandma, and here I was provided with the tools given to her. They are useful but they were not enough.

My birth mother, though a kind person, lingers broken in the wings of life, transferring her energy into me like we are still connected at the umbilical cord. I am her: face, body, actions, desperately clinging on to the hopes of my life, while staying stagnant in the past of my broken heart. Believing and struggling to mend the broken pieces of the little girl who was loved, but not the way she needed to be.

My dad, I met him once when I was twenty-three. He, on his deathbed, lying there looking like a piece of glass rock, covered in the sorrows of a drunken stupor, his hand so puffy that I couldn't resist touching it. Where the nurse called me brave because I embraced his lifeless body, and I hopelessly wanted to bring him back to life so I could forge a memory other than this one. I associate death with him, and therefore my memory serves as a constant reminder that the little girl in me will never get the chance to know him.

A cracked, fragile girl, just gasping for air. Rebuilding dreams. Still struggling to feel like a woman.

My brother's dad. He's the epitome of baseness. I believed for a long time that I was making stories up. I'm good at making shit up, but who wants to write about their mother being hit over the head with a lamp pole? Who wants to write about not being able to breathe because he couldn't understand that a little girl with asthma needed her inhaler? I'd like to forget. I'd like to believe that parts of my childhood were a comic book I made up in my head. But I'm not a fool. I can still spot the clown in plain sight.

Why should I pick myself back up again? Why should I take the tools they have given me and forge them into adaptations that fit my needs? To live and enjoy this life I'm currently living. So, answering the question on everyone's lips.

11

Grammy

My grandma lay in a bed like a bus stop, waiting
for Jesus to come, and she became softer when
she was no longer in control. Her vulnerability
peeled itself off the floor and presented itself to
her. Since I'd known her, this was the first time I
saw her give permission to herself to be 'weak'
and that's when I noticed her strengths.

She could no longer hide behind the cloak of the
garment she had used to protect herself.
Bending at the mercy of the
universe—preemptively giving her the
opportunity to transform. I found the
metamorphosis beautiful.

Silently sitting. I always wondered if she felt
trapped in her mind, even though she kept a
smile on her face, if the magnitude of her life was
playing on repeat while her voice had been
stripped away from her. I speculated as to
whether she felt like she gave up too soon, as if
trying one more thing in this lifetime would be
way too much for her to handle.

And maybe it was... I went on loving her as
though nothing had ever changed.

She had that effect on me... on many of us, really.
I don't remember the sound of her voice.

But what it gave in the interim was how I solidified what truly loving people felt like.
Her voice was loud in her warm embraces, in her boisterous laughs that almost always ended in coughs. Her smile was a warmth to my seemingly cloudy late teens and early twenties.

The bus finally arrived at her stop, and I understand now that watching her leaning into her softness means more to me today than it ever could've then.
She stays with many of us. Some wonderful memories... some not so much... but that's the beauty of love... and loss.

My Mother Is A Mystery

My mother is a mystery.

Her dark brown eyes hide the passions that she's afraid to seek. Strong in her convictions, her love is unchanging.

The little girl attached to her hip, the little boy affixed to her presence. Does she miss her adolescence?

Black beauty, shedding her skin in preparation to present herself anew so the world may know...

Dial back the education... Education of a world that encapsulated her, hid her within the bosom of its comfort, but left her malnourished enough to make her hunger for more.

Standing on a trapeze, trying to complete the balancing act that was unconsciously handed to her.

Exemplifying the radiance of motherhood, while harmonizing the correlations of being not only a mother but a woman. How mingled the two have become for her...

Salted wounds mended by the broken-hearted cries and the impromptu worship ceremonies in her bedroom... Boy...

My mother is a mystery.

Reflecting her impatience, life is moving too slow,
yet moving too fast all on the same note…

A woman who's never been an open book, but
not really a completely closed one either.

My mother is a mystery.

I watch her peer at herself in the mirror, and I
pause… I take in the moment of her natural
beauty… The strength that dangles from her
head to her ankles… The little girl that longs to
know the truth… The nostalgia in her mind,
replaying the memories of what was and
daydreaming of what could've been. I see
myself… ·

However, my mother is still a mystery.

A Mother's Religion

My momma is a praying woman.

A woman of worship and fervent energy to serve a God so willing to give her her heart's desires, as long as she followed in his will. And even when she failed, he would always remain faithful. After all, he's a promise keeper.

My momma is a praying woman.

And as I watched her cling on to the hope that God would make a way of restoring my grandma's health and the conversation amongst us progressed, I told her that God was no longer a part of me, and I watched her heart sink… her face washed over with confusion.

In a room that seemed to suck the air right out of me, I glanced at my grandma and saw her eyes dance to the rhythm of our ancestors… or maybe it was just my imagination, hoping that someone in the room was fighting for me.

My momma is a praying woman.

Still in her prayer closet, wrapping the universe in a God energy that even in my disbelief still coats me with the protection of her words. Embodying the spirit of God that allows her to love me just as I am. Her daughter.

My momma is a praying woman.

A prayer warrior raised and perhaps born to battle the universe in her own right. She has the freedom of choice, too, so she taught me the value of those praying for me. When she prays for me, that's her way of showing me love, her own particular way of breathing life into me. And if I learned to let people love me in their own spiritual ways, then I'd know the love of the universe.

My momma is a praying woman.

Pressing into what lies ahead, and never letting go of the promise that God will never fail her. Because the promise keeper's love will never fail. And though our beliefs are not the same, I know the universe will continue teaching us the art of hearing each other's cries, building an undeniable love that is true and unfailing.

Truth Dance

I danced a dance amongst some truths today, and I wondered how my knees have survived this long.

How demons chose the melody, but my heart danced to its own rhythm.

I danced a dance amongst my story today, and I wondered how I waltzed between the raindrops, catching just enough water to soak into my soul.

Fascinated that the pillars in my life have stayed this strong. Endured unspoken storms and yet their tears watered seeds being produced today.

I danced a dance amongst some truths today, and rejoiced in the spoken and unspoken victories that surfaced some paths for me to walk and conquer.

I danced a dance amongst intertwined stories today, and I twirl with thanks, knowing I have come from and have been raised by strong women.

The melody changes as I dance my dance amongst portions of our stories today.

Ancestor Strong

I sit here strong...
Cloaked in an armor I never asked to bear.
My ancestors passed it down to me as if it was an heirloom.
I breathe in the strength that they had to lean into.

I stand still, marking the creases of my brain in the memory that this encounter is what I'd have of you. Your body, almost devoid of oxygen, lay limp, trying to hold on to all the love in the room. It wasn't enough for your survival. It was a hello and a goodbye, almost an homage to how we first met.

I sit here strong...
Cloaked in an armor I never asked to bear.
My ancestors passed it down to me, like old photos etched into the fabric of my being.
The strength they had to hold... holds me.

A descendant of slaves, burying their souls, hoping to know their dreams could blossom. For this moment, I lie perched on the couch, pondering the gratitude of my being... of their survival... of the cloaked armor passed down to me unconsciously.
How much lighter it feels to carry it, even in the wake of knowing how heavy it truly is.

The pressure of the world mounts itself onto my shoulders as I'm thrusted from my cocoon. The force of natural agency pushes me to lean into the hard things.
This intensity sometimes makes me cling to this armor while I try to catch my breath.

I sit here strong...
Cloaked in an armor none of us asked to bear.
Here, I take a deep breath...
I'll move vulnerably this time. I'll place perimeters and boundaries to avoid massive damage, but I'll choose to be strong differently. Because of my ancestors, I can.

Reflections: ... Give You Something To Cry About

Reflecting on your parents when writing can bring bittersweet emotions. Sometimes the feelings linger long after the poem has escaped my body and made its way into my pen or has become an electronic document. I grew up in a small, close-knit family and community, built by the hands of Black men and women alike. I grew up in a holy home, an unapologetically Black home. The Black experience is knitted into my experiences and DNA all the same. The poems in this section all stem from various moments throughout my life, reflections on some of my most daunting yet most beautiful moments of clarity. In hindsight, these moments played major roles in the woman I've become, and they have yielded much insight into the woman I want to be.

A Letter To My Father:
I wrote this letter in December 2013. I wrote this letter to my father, hoping to build a relationship with him. If there was any shame attached to my adoption, or him not stepping up to help prevent it, I was ready to move forward, because it was overall a great thing that happened. At the time of writing the letter, I had talked to him on the phone three times after reconnecting with my biological family in 2009. Each time we spoke it was fairly short, like he was in a rush, but the day

21

of this letter was a little different. We talked for about an hour. He told me about my football team of siblings and how he wanted to meet me soon. That day came, but it wasn't like either of us imagined it would be, as reflected in Little Girl and Ancestor Strong.

Little Girl:
I wrote this poem in reflection on my experience, on parts of the Black experience, where systematic oppression required my adoptive mom to be gone for double shifts in order to take care of her family as a single mother. It's a reflection of how my biological mother and I share similar traits, and how being loved is enough until it's not—not enough for what we needed to feel okay with who we are in the world. It's a reflection of how life is short and the relationship I longed to have with my dad would never occur in the way I'd envisioned. It was the healing in acknowledging that my experiences are just that... and I didn't need to have them validated for them to be true. This poem was hard for me to write and, if I'm being transparent, harder for me to share here with you all. Sometimes it takes us to reflect on where and who we come from in order to heal and in some ways to help them heal too. Seeing my parents as humans instead of people who were perfect helped me find some grace. It's been hard in spaces, but beautiful in some too.

Grammy:
I wrote the poem Grammy long after I had lost her. Over the course of her life and mine intermingling, she became my best friend, I suppose like many of us in the Black community, where elders can be a refuge. Though we became best friends, we weren't always that way. We fought. I thought she was mean sometimes. And she was. She had been sick twice over, but this time was different. She softened in a way that allowed me to see her humanness. It lended way to her, giving me her heart in such a different way that when I had to go through my own storms later on in life, I had some tools that helped me soften too. I'm forever grateful for her lessons, not only from the grave but from her time here on earth.

My Mother Is A Mystery:
I began writing this poem as I was deep in thought about my mother, about how she's aging, about how much she's given up in her lifetime, about how much of her and her life still felt mysterious to me. How I could see the stories draping from her body, but they appeared to be written in a foreign language so I couldn't understand. I've found that many Black mothers are this way, so I'm learning to create a haven for mine without the fear of shame or guilt. I observed what I knew about her, how she was blossoming and cocooning (what seemed to be)

all at the same time. As our relationship is blooming, so is my knowledge of her, and I'll be forever grateful to be the preserver of her stories.

A Mother's Religion:
As I mentioned above, I grew up in a holy home. For most of my life, I carried God with me. I still carry various pieces of Christianity with me. I wrote this poem after I told my mom that I no longer believed in her God. Being religious was so embedded in her teachings for me, it was one of the hardest things I had to do in my twenties. I had to walk through being okay with the possibility of her not accepting me, but learned that she loved me regardless. It's funny how our own perceptions can stop us from having hard yet necessary conversations.

Truth Dance:
Mother's Day, mid pandemic, I called my mothers up and burrowed down into the truth of my life, of their lives. I learned lessons about how I was brought into this world, and how my life changed in such a small amount of time. I was in awe of the resilience I heard from my mothers and was invigorated that I come from so much love and strength.

Ancestor Strong:
My husband and I went down the rabbit hole of ancestry.com and started piecing my family tree together. In doing so, I learned about my family

roots, about how some of them were slaves, about how they migrated for safety and personal reasons. I faced learning about some of their untimely deaths due to the paths some of them had chosen (or had been given, depending on who's telling the tale). In doing so, I started thinking about my dad, whom I'd met as he was taking his last breath, and I became overwhelmingly grateful for the strength in all their stories, ones that have helped catapult my life forward. I wrote this poem in honor of that.

Undelivered Blueprint

TimeStamp

There's a time stamp on my marriage.
Not the traditional one, where you grow old
together and the heartbreak is of the natural
kind. See, there's a time stamp on my marriage.
One-hundred-eighty-one days.
two-hundred-forty four minutes… sounds like
an eternity when I put it that way, doesn't it? A
timestamp that dictates if patience is really a
virtue… if growing apart is really synonymous
with the happiness we are both seeking.

There's a time stamp on my marriage.
I mean… the problems aren't that bad. It's
simply whether or not one can catch up to the
other in hopes of bridging the gap that divides
the portal of open communication. We are
constantly on different wavelengths, missing the
frequency of each other's heartbeat, forgetting
that, most days, the rhythm should be
synchronized. A timestamp like touching is a
foreign language we just can't seem to get a grasp
on.

There's a time stamp on my marriage. Like the
milk in the back of the fridge we bought to satisfy
our need for creamy tea and the little bit of cereal
we had left, thinking, "I'm going to finish that,"
but then it sits in the back of the fridge and we
forget about it. The expiration date came before

we knew it. And I don't want my marriage to be like this metaphorical analogy.

There's a timestamp on my marriage.
I don't want that manufactured, packaged love. I want love so fresh that I can pick it off the tree and determine whether it's good or bad, and even if it's bad I can still make a delicious pie out of it. The good and the bad are intertwined and that's the kind of love I want... not all good, not all bad, but both. See the roots of the tree have produced both good and bad but it doesn't mean that the tree is rotten. Love is like that!

We come from two different places, spaces, backgrounds, and ideologies. Some good, some bad, and the roots that we create together are not going to create good fruit all the time. But that doesn't make the experience of picking a fresh fruit off the tree not worth it.

I hope the time stamp on my marriage gets revised back to its original deadline, where love is always and forever... until death do us part... until the sun can shine no longer because even though fairy tales don't exist, I still want to be his Cinderella, and he my prince charming.

Wounded Together - Fuck The Fairytale

Us, on our own battlefields converging together in hopes of making the war less painful. Seemingly buried in the trenches of life, expecting to be covered enough from the stray bullets flying towards us.

Drenched in emotional war traumas experienced throughout our personal combat missions. We tried to find our way out, but instead found ourselves wounded together.

Tied by the heartstrings of being able to clearly see one another. We tried our damnedest to stitch up each other's lacerations to get us to a place of comfort. Unknowingly leaving the wound open enough to affect how we walked through life.

Where peace fades into the background and is a distant memory in this war zone. Where the dusted atmosphere drowns the clarity of a positive outcome of where we'll be next.

Fighting soul wounds that we watched our parents unsuccessfully battle through. Marred by the subtleties of our wounds seeping their poison into our most sacred spaces. Our foundation is now infected and must be cleansed to save it.

Our own guns cocked, seeing each other as the enemy. Those rose-colored spectacles now tainted, we were holding heavy rifles and shooting friendly fire. Wondering where the hell our relief in each other went. Gunshot wound-riddled hearts, induced into surgery with no anesthesia to mask the pain any longer. Now disconnected in what was supposed to be our fairytale—facing our own wars head-on in hopes that we come out champions and our battle scars are more of a lesson than a burden. In hopes that the PTSD of our past dissipates as we heal after surgery. That this is just the ordeal of our hero's journey, trudging along, and we'll end up converging together as individuals to help make each other stronger.

We are wounded together, healing in our own spaces. So fuck the fairytale we somehow figured we'd get, and let's write our own badass, powerful story.

My Love. This Love. Our Love.

Some days you are like a gunshot wound to the chest. You've taken my breath away. You've somehow married our religions and then obliterated them just for the sake of loving me. If you hadn't taught me how to love like this, I would have had to learn how to lather my own body with compliments, like the ones that come so easily from your lips. I'd have to complete an open-heart surgery. I would have to saturate my skin in a bank of google searches, hoping to find a more efficient way to make my heart flutter. A gunshot wound to the chest that has taken my breath away.

When we got married, I wrote my worries in the creases of my mind, bottled up my fears, hoping that you'd hear them through my silence. That your love for me would transcend the uneasiness of what has been called 'the best day of a woman's life.' That you are the sunshine in a cloud of stormy times. I genuinely wrapped myself into the love you were giving me. Your love has always been like a gunshot wound to the chest, always taking my breath away.

Our love, a crescendo ricocheting off the inner walls of my heart, whispering that even in the hard times, we'd be okay. Feeling the balance between the sun touching the leaves and the rain nourishing them after a long sunshine. The brilliance of our hearts opening up, and the contingency of letting mine drop to the cement in hopes that it still has some bounce left.

This is my love… our love… a crescendo… like a gunshot wound to the chest, ricocheting off the inner walls of my heart.

Some days life is like a gunshot wound to the chest. It will take our breath away, piercing our deepest fears so that we must undergo our own personal surgeries in hopes of healing and uncovering a life that we never knew imaginable. Where I'd have to lather my own body with my own sultry compliments, opening my mouth so that the silence doesn't drown me… us… you… so that my heart flutters with and without you. So that we are alive and healing… alive and breathing… alive and seen. A gunshot wound to the chest, but this time it will teach us to breathe new life into the universe. Separately and unified and, to me, that breath is more precious than anything. My love… our love… this love… like a gunshot wound to the chest, ricocheting off the inner walls of our hearts.

Orbital Rotation

I got lost in his orbit. He Jupiter, I Saturn.

Neither of our moons occupied by something more than each other. His gravitational pull was electrifying. I gave in to his power without even asking if he could bear the extra load. His orbital resonance, consistent with mine, has periodically, over the years, formed celestial bodies, developed to interlock the behaviors of our combined orbits around the sun. Spawning a double-edged sword to de-establish a married cultural system, yet locking our magnetic powers into stability. Tides locking our co-orbiting astronomical bodies so much that we have achieved the orbital eccentricity of synchronous rotation. We are officially lost in orbit together.

He Jupiter, I Saturn. Neither of our moons occupied by something more than each other. My gravitational pull was liberating. He gave in to my influence without realizing how much of an effect I'd have on his nature. Our satellites in orbital rotation, a sequenced one-year revolution around the sun captured the attention of a newfound scientist discovering affection.

They realize love is synonymous with the universe. At that very moment, they understand.

He Jupiter, I Saturn. And neither of our moons occupied by something more than each other.

Je T'aime Pour Toujours

With far-fetched dreams so grandiose, we
snuggle into the comfort of wanting to know
each other most.

Though life's natural storms may sometimes
destroy our scenery, let's ride this
communication boat and create new meanings.

Sculpting our new landscapes and inventing new
ways to stay nourished. Combating behaviors
that let weeds flourish. And as we become more
planted in love, may our grounded palm trees
sway freely in the breeze as a gentle reminder
that nothing beautiful comes with ease.

May our mountains steal our breaths away, but in
the best kind of 'I can't breathe' way. Reminding
us that our doormat is the only thing allowed to
remain scuffed and dirty. And that our
prism-glassed home will continually be shattered
each and every time we dream together.
Synching the boundaries of the love we create
can be endless, if only we authorize them to be.

Our far-fetched dreams so grandiose, we snuggle
into the comfort of loving each other most.

Reflections: Undelivered Blueprint

Getting married is one of the biggest commitments one can make in their lives. I made that commitment at eighteen-years-old. My husband is my best friend and we have been married for over a decade now. The hardest thing about two kids coming from poverty and not seeing healthy marriages growing up is that we've had to figure out a great deal of this thing called 'marriage' on our own. Over the course of our decade of marriage together, we've laughed, we've cried, we've fought (unfairly sometimes), we've grown, and we've loved each other through it all. The poems in this section reflect that. This section reflects the pain of feeling like we were going to end our relationship, it reflects the knowledge and grace that we had to learn and are learning to give to one another as we unearth our traumas and work through them. It reflects that he is my best friend and that he has had (and still does have) a great effect on my life. We didn't have a blueprint, so we're making it up as we go. Which means we've gotten a lot of things right and some things wrong, and we're learning when and where to adjust in the ways that best suit us as a unit.

TimeStamp:
TimeStamp was written during a time in my marriage where I thought we were going to end it all. Where growing pains were weighing on us

heavily and we couldn't see how we'd come out of the fog. We set a deadline on how long we'd be willing to keep holding onto each other during this growing season. This poem helped me get the BIG emotions out. It helped me put some things into perspective. It helped me cope while we were trying to figure out how to move forward.

Wounded Together - Fuck the Fairytale:
Wounded Together came about after I had restarted my therapy journey. We had just moved to Denver, and for the first time in our marriage we were not close to our village. These two things combined stirred up those emotions of, "Oh wow! We've hurt each other unintentionally, but here we were trying to stay connected while healing our own shit." It wasn't easy to feel distant from my love and best friend, and this poem I believe reflects the idea of processing my own trauma while trying to do our very best to hold onto one another—even when everything felt like it was falling apart. It's a reflection of how we are trying to dismantle bad behaviors and patterns we've carried with us and figuring out how to disregard the 'fairytale' of marriage that we received when we were younger. It grounded me in knowing that we aren't perfect, but if we both put in work, there's nothing we can't do.

My Love. This Love. Our Love.:
This poem emerged as I was reflecting on my marriage. We had eloped. The day we married in the courthouse, I was scared, I was happy, I was sure yet unsure. I was so in awe of how my husband had learned to love me, even in some of the craziest moments, and how even though we didn't have examples of marriage, his love carried me most days, a love that would always stick in my memory regardless of how difficult it got. It was a reminder to myself that marriage wouldn't always feel so hard.

Orbital Rotation:
Orbital Rotation is the nerd in me shining! This poem was written in honor of the fact that my husband is a huge science geek. It was a part of an anniversary present I gave him. This poem challenged me to learn and understand how we are connected at such a level that we will always pull each other closer and, somehow, we'll always figure out how to love each other better.

Je T'aime Pour Toujours:
Je T'aime Pour Toujours (I love you forever) is a poem that I wrote for our eleven-year anniversary. I was reflecting on how beautiful and powerful our love has been and is continuing to be, that our dreams aren't too big if we lean into one another and trust each other's strengths. It was a moment of leaning into

understanding that he is and has always been my person.

What Happens In This House...

A Black American Dad Story

June 4th, you showed up as though you have been present the entire time. The awkwardness you have brought with you could be cut with my knifed tongue, struggling to avoid creating tension. I promised myself that my brother's day wouldn't be clouded by your reappearance, that your magic trick wasn't tricking anyone anymore.

Graduation day, an accomplishment not only his but also our mother's, her succeeding in helping him construct his own path without you. See, our mother is the nice one here. Because if it were up to me, just like your lack of existence in his life, the invitation in your mailbox wouldn't have been present either. You, too, would have clicked play on a video like the rest of the world, being able to only congratulate him through a pixelated version of your eighteen years of missed experiences.

Here, from my seat at the table, I'm boiling over with delusion because there is no possible way that we are sitting here listening to stories about you! My face says it all, scrunched up into a look that is so unapologetically throat-slitting, I can't believe I haven't willed you to stop talking with just my facial expression. It's evident from your lack of celebration that you showed up to get praise and glory that don't really belong to you. You've acted like you had amnesia until you needed him. And, somehow, you've managed to claim yourself as a victim in a room full of slaughtered hopes, dreams and memories, while you boldly stand here holding the machete that robbed ALL of your children from knowing you. We are all uncomfortable.

I butt in and sway the conversation back to the man of the hour. This celebratory dinner is almost over. My brother leaves quickly from this encounter, so much so that he forgets to hug me goodbye. I look at graduation pictures now and wonder how much photoshop magic I'll have to learn in order to erase you. Because your presence does not deserve to be a part of this accomplishment. This moment. This memory.

This Black American dad story from my seat at the table reminds me that my brother looks exactly like you, but fortunately for those of us who know him, your heart will never match the one beating within him. One day he'll be able to repair the missing spaces of his broken heart, when he begins to recreate the story of the Black American dad that you just couldn't be. Perhaps from your absence he'll have learned that his #blackboyjoy lies within his emotions, and that to truly overcome this curse is to not be afraid to face them. May he break down the egotistical barricades that you buried within his DNA. And when he looks in the mirror, may he be reminded that he has the divine opportunity to generate a new generation of children who know the love of their father.

Here, from my seat at the table, this Black American dad story conceivably has some added hope.

My Brother!

"My brother!" I proclaim to the world, as though he is the only one. I marvel at your stature as you've grown tall from the ten-year-old boy who did not yet understand that his dreams could be as big as the world. Benevolence lingers on your skin as you traverse through the murky waters of young manhood.

"My brother!" I proclaim to the world, as though he is the only one. Ominous signals sent to capture his attention in hopes that he detects their urgency. He scurries with his thoughts of finding himself… loving who he is… embracing his truths… all the while, my smoke signals go unnoticed.

"My brother!" I proclaim to the world, as though he is the only one. The world is consumed by more than just collecting a coin, flexing with your boys, and coping the Afrocentric girl with the coke bottle shape you see at the mall. A scrunched face exclaims that he doesn't want to hear it.

"My brother!" I proclaim to the world, as though he is the only one. Kiss the sun, embrace the earth, marvel in the beauty of humanity and be provoked by the injustices that capture those who resemble you. Humans, that is. I embellish and reflect on what Forrest Gump said, that "life is like a box of chocolates, you never know what you're going to get." But the box clearly states the contents inside. "Life isn't so kind," I explain.

"My brother!" I proclaim to the world, as though he is the only one. Young man, your scraped knee is immeasurable to your broken heart. When falling off your bike with no helmet on feels better than being alone with yourself. Contemplation increases as you tangle your experiences together.

"My brother!" I proclaim to the world, as though he is the only one. I see the intricacies of your mind, forcing you to catch a breath. It's uncomfortable, you can't breathe in the suffocation of living in someone else's shadow. You must not relinquish your power. You are a king and your crown awaits…

"My brother!" I proclaim to the world, as though he is the only one.

Destitute

Overwhelmed.

How many times can we talk about being homeless? Focusing on going into people's homes in hopes that they won't release you back into the wilderness where the wolves will no doubt feed on you.

How many times do I advocate for the good in you before you see it too?

Overwhelmed.

The systemically-wrapped ties around your wrist and ankles, I can't even be mad at you. But I can push you to break free.

Overwhelmed.

How many times can I offer you a path out of a perpetual cycle, and you not take it?

Defeated.

Ping! Your distress signal dings. I don't open it to avoid my emotions shifting.

Self-protection.

I don't pray, but if I did, I'd want God to respond to my request with the speed of light. I'd pray that you'd soften in the right spaces, that you'd let love—true healthy love—grow over those weeded spaces, and you'd thrive. I'd pray that you'd always feel like enough because you always have been. I'd pray for your safety, but most importantly for a healed recovery from a life that was systematically and emotionally suppressive. Maybe I'd use my cries for the universe this time too, just covering all the bases.

Overwhelmed but hopeful.

Are You Okay?

People kept asking if I was okay.
"Yea, I'm alright," I'd reply.
They'd retort with, "You don't have to hold it in."
I'd strongly reply, "I'm alright!"

See what they don't understand is the number
eight. I've prepared for this moment—as much as
one ever could—and I took that time to love her.
When my best friend was no longer just a
bedroom away, scanning the channels, looking
for a distraction.

I spent my time probing her mind, when she
would allow it. And making her sure that my love
for her would never fail. Eight… the number of
years I spent my time frolicking on the swings
with her, as she sat confined to her chair and
never letting go of her hugs and, if I let go too
soon, always being sure to go back for another.
Boy, I loved her so. This is what withholds me.
"Now, never did I say this was not difficult… I
said I was alright," I proclaim, as I am continually
reminded by this conversation that I no longer
had her.

Singing in my head the song that seemed to hold
me together at the moment: "There are three
things I do when my life falls apart! Number one,
I cry my eyes out and dry up my heart, not until I
do this will my new life start, and that's the first

thing that I do when my life falls apart." In perspective, I had cried my eyes out many years before; many hospital visits in a chair, her eyes closed, mine cloudy with fear, knowing that this moment was near. Eight times... eight years.... and only three people shared in my intimate outburst of anger that I'd no longer get to love on her and be loved by her in only the way she could.

People kept asking me if I was okay.
"Yea, I'm alright," I'd reply.
They'd retort with, "You don't have to hold it in, ya know."
I'd strongly reply, "I'm alright!"

In my mind, I reason with what I just said: I'm alright because I have a cornucopia of memories and an uncharted belief in knowing she wanted two grandkids from me, instead of my highly-suggested one. Mostly, I'm alright because she knew I was happy... I was shaped in the imagery of her beauty. I clung to her like a leaf to your raincoat in the fall. I no longer had her earthly vessel, but I understood she'd forever be present in my memories!

People kept asking me if I was okay.
"Yea, I'm alright" I'd reply.

I ponder momentarily. "She's at peace now. She can speak freely now with the earth as though her breath was never stolen. She can kiss me on the cheeks when she assists the sun in rising. She can still embrace me when she tucks me in at night and meets me in my dreams. She'll keep the stars sparkling, just for me, just to remind me that even the dimmest light shines bright enough for someone else to see. Yea, I'm alright, because she lives within me."

Mirror

I look in the mirror and I do not see myself.

I see a blurred image of a woman who once existed and, further in the distance, a grained image of the one I'm destined to become.

I look in the mirror and I do not see myself.

I see the lashes of life that have caused callused bruises to rise and blister at the sight of any opposition. No matter what stage of the game I'm in, I'm playing defense.

I look in the mirror and I do not see myself.

Therapeutic Thoughts

Deep dive into this sea of forgiveness,
Wrapped in the contentment of wanting to just
be comfortable.

Fist swinging…
Slow breathing…
I can't believe I've lived through this…

These…
Those…
Experiences…

Oxygen depleted veins seeping poison into my
body the longer I decided I didn't have the
capacity to face my giants.

I was afraid of the dark until I realized I was the
light.

See Me

Sea salted wounds heighten my will to want to be
seen perfectly. Ears enclosed by headphones.
How am I being seen? Can I sit here and pretend
to have it figured out, or lay bare in the fact that
I'm just wasting time?

How am I being seen?

The sound of silence fills the room and I wonder.
A conversation with myself about myself…
How do I see… me? The echo of the fridge
intensifies, engulfs me in the rhythmic pulses of
trying to find its own heartbeat.

Just like me I suppose.

I lay flat on my back. Took a deep breath.
Maybe just one more. Sink myself into the floor.
Let the perfectionism wound lay open, let the
chill of the wind hit it.

I breathe.

My heart beats.

I cry a deep cry.

Vulnerable Submission

I sat on a bench and watched my body detach from itself as I submitted to the act of vulnerability.

Surrounded by my tribe of women cheering for me, caring for me, and some praying for me, even when I didn't want them to.

Sitting here in a suspended state, I understood tearfully that change of any kind required grace, and change meant I needed to be vulnerable.

Vulnerability began pushing on my heart and sprung forth an urgency from my once quiet murmurs, and I realized that to be at peace is an art form.

Pursuing a diligent attitude in keeping up as thoughts cascade in and out of consciousness. Chiseling through a mind that hadn't stopped to breathe or function in the love I so freely give to others.

A compressed acceptance of my personal changes because I thought that those I love wouldn't love me anymore. It yielded a mental feeling of loneliness, which turned into a perception of being incapable.

I was stripping myself to appease and provide peace to those engaged in my life. Vulnerability standing firm in now teaching me that it's okay to be seen. Gently reminding me that change requires peace. So I found the key to my brain, unlocked the door and gave myself permission to live. I gave myself permission to be vulnerable, permission to truly be seen, permission to genuinely be loved by those who know the real me.

I sat on a bench and watched my body reattach itself as I submitted to the act of vulnerability. Now understanding that this change will require my own grace, and often the willingness to submit to the act of vulnerability.

Undecided Indecisive

As the sun sets and rises, I find my strength stuck in the mango tree above. Yonder I see the tide roaring, ushering in the hurricane that whispers, "I'm baaaack!"

I mentally begin to panic.
Knowing—feeling, rather—that I'm not going to survive. I slap myself back and forth a few times until I conjure up the strength that I locked in my coconut bag marked 'adulthood.'

I was ready!
I was afraid.
I had absolutely no idea what lay ahead of me.
But I needed to do it.

I wanted to meet everyone on the other side.
I wanted to be in love, *real* love, and I wanted to be openly understanding of it.
I wanted to talk freely, love kindly, and be happy with myself.

By now the tide was rolling in faster and I had to make my decision quickly: was I going to drown, or could I use the utensils in my makeshift tool bag to carry me to safety?

Healing Emotions

It grows heavy when the trauma smacks you in the face again after you've managed to suppress all these emotions. Unintentionally... intentionally... maybe a bit of both.

Like a weighted blanket lay heavy on me. Rivers flowing from my eyes, watering the seeds of the good I did, trying to grow over the weeds that lie dormant here. Somehow, they coexist. Simply tired, I lie here.

What happens when these emotions won't let rest find me? When the words don't spill out of the pen as fast as they roam around in my head?

I deep breathe.

When sixty minutes isn't enough time to break down each thought with your therapist, but the release of these few, just for the moment, will do.

I'm still lying here. Thinking... staring at the ceiling...

I've managed these emotions over the years through hidden poetry books, silent tears, eight+ hours of pixelated distractions, many poured whiskey glasses masked in wanting to have a good time. Management for only the heavy ones, I suppose.

The good emotions sometimes linger for just a moment, so I'm practicing how not to forebode my joy so the heaviness of healing doesn't suffocate me in my sleep.

I breathe… release…

I listen with my knowing, and my best kept secret is that I can't always manage. It's all in the trying. It's in riding the tides of the ocean but somehow never letting them consume me completely.

I breathe…
My emotions are magic.
I finally rest.

Broken-Hearted Syndrome

As I take stock of my life, I notice the multitude of broken pieces. I do not possess black magic. I am no sorcerer. But I need to conjure up the spirits, for these broken pieces can surely become a different masterpiece.

These broken-hearted fragments adrift in the wind, being carried from one anchor in my life to another, undocking the peace of my mind and experiences.

The flood of anxiety seeps through my blood, and the falsehoods of my words penetrate my veins with enough poison to kill me.

My heart slows to an unhealthy beat, and I feel my lungs collapsing. Symptoms of broken-hearted syndrome, triggered by my own death.

Now, cocooning out of my shell, trying to understand the woman I've become. Examining the vast backdrop of my life in hopes to retrieve the wisdom I so absent-mindedly left behind.

Struggling so desperately to master the woman I've become. Learning how to allow myself to be free from the past, and authentically letting myself be free enough to change, free enough to

say *no* and free enough to tell someone to *back
the hell up* when I am feeling invaded.

I look at the broken pieces of my life again and I
noticed they've rearranged themselves.
This time the picture is much clearer, showing
the mountains I have conquered, encouraging me
to keep embracing a daily practice of letting go,
marveling in the beauty that is my life and
realizing that without the pain I wouldn't know
the joy.

And though sorrow is always one knock away in
this life, I'll choose to continue my journey with
my head high, red-lipped and unapologetic
because, after all, queens run villages too.

Reflections: What Happens In This House...

Growing up in a Black family, it was always said, "What happens in this house, stays in this house." Growing up in a low-income household that was redlined and located in a food desert didn't exactly provide the best of opportunities for me or those who looked like me to receive the mental help that comes with going to therapy. In hindsight, I'm realizing that the "what happens in this house" statement was just a way to hide what made us and our parents feel shame. When in a healthy environment, shame cannot thrive. These poems are a reflection of different phases in my life when things felt unfair, tough, shameful, vulnerable, and hard. They represent my need to always release and feel in order to reflect.

A Black American Dad Story:
This poem was hard yet very easy for me to write. I've always been the protective big sister. Leading up to this day of celebration I felt a little out of place being the one to help navigate and coordinate with my brother's dad about details for the event. This was in order to help ensure my mom's peace of mind at the time. After all was said and done, I was flooded with so many emotions that I had to sit down and write them all out. I've shared this poem during open mic nights and on my personal social media pages

and have gotten tons of responses from people with similar experiences. It helped me realize that my words have power.

My Brother:
My brother and I have been building our adult relationship for a while now. When he was younger, I wanted to download everything I had learned about the world into him. Being seven years older, I've had to learn how to dial back what I share, and most of the time that results in me writing it out. I wanted to encourage him, to warn him, and to protect him, all in the same breath. It's hard watching him become a man, but I know it is necessary to let him soar.

Destitute:
I wrote this poem in a session in Chicago where the topic of the evening was focused on managing our emotions. The person in this poem was so heavy on my mind that I felt I needed to write about the perpetual cycle she finds herself in, and the one her and I were creating as siblings. I had to release the emotion of my superhero complex and allow, in some ways, for life to play out but also to be okay with providing guidance in some spaces.

Are You Okay?:
This poem was written almost a year after I had lost my grammy. I was still processing. I was still coming to peace with it all. In writing it out, I got

the opportunity to expand and explain my emotions, and it helped provide a better way of processing the loss I had experienced.

Mirror:
Mirror was birthed during a reflective time in my life. One morning I was looking in the mirror and I didn't recognize the woman looking back at me. I had to acknowledge how I was living defensively in my life and I wanted to change that. Going to therapy has helped me acknowledge my triggers and allows me the opportunity to see my growth, not just over time but in real time as well.

Therapeutic Thoughts:
Therapeutic Thoughts was my outlet to help release suppressed emotions I was holding. It helped me understand that I had not forgiven myself or certain people in my life because I wasn't ready. Seeing the feelings and emotions written down allowed me the opportunity to start working through forgiving not only people in my life, but myself as well.

See Me:
As an adopted child, Black woman and oldest daughter, I've always wanted to be seen perfectly. Like I was the right loaf of bread off the top shelf. I wanted the world I was in to think I had it all figured out. I've let go of a lot of trying to be perfect or appear perfect. Some days I still

struggle with the perfection perception piece, but I'm learning. Therapy is helping me cultivate a new habit in understanding that nothing is perfect and I am no exception.

Vulnerable Submission:
Vulnerability was not something taught when I was growing up. Vulnerability was seen mostly as a weakness. In this poem, I express how I realized I was being a people pleaser and I was setting myself on fire in order to make other people comfortable, and I wanted to stop doing that. In transitioning into being seen, I've had to learn to show myself compassion and grace in those moments where I'd much rather lean into being harsher with myself or more of a people pleaser.

Undecided Indecisive:
As I reflect on this poem, I realize that I was afraid of moving forward. I was nervous that I wouldn't be able to grow and shift in the ways that I thought necessary. I had been in therapy for several months at this point, but I still wasn't confident in the tools I had gained to move forward.

Healing Emotions:
I wrote this poem from a prompt, one that made me reflect on my emotions of healing and how I take care of myself. I was learning how to rest my mind and body, but always seemed unable to. I

still struggle with this sometimes, but I'm
becoming more okay with resting.

Broken-Hearted Syndrome:
This poem was birthed when I was reflecting on
my life. I was fired from my job and realized that
I had been carrying so much of my old self into
so many new spaces that required me to do
something other than survive. During this
moment, I felt like I had missed out on so much
of my own growth and understood that I would
never get to a place where I wasn't aware of
myself anymore.

WILDLIFE

WildFire

As we drive through the fires of the Utah deserts,
I feel my body fueling the flame of my emotions.

A bright sunny day, ever so clear, can become
foggy and immersive with just one spark of
influence. Sometimes by my own natural force,
and other times by the hands of strangers.

Just like the fire, I am burning my own paths and
breaking down the resistant barriers that deny
me the right to be wildly free.

And though I'm aware that the smoke I have
created hides the mountains I may need to climb,
I'll pack my oxygen mask and trek on. Because I
know beyond those mountains are more paths
for me to help clear out spaces for others to
grow.

I am the spark, and I am the fire!

Replenished Duality

Sometimes we flourish in the forest.
Sometimes we shed ourselves and close our eyes
for a while to replenish.

Both beaming with life.
One knowing it's time to shed and the other
understanding it's time to shine.

The duality amongst shedding and shining.
Giving and taking. Leaning in and standing tall.
Knowing when to rest and when to dance.

Sometimes we flourish in the forest.
Sometimes we shed and close our eyes for a
while to replenish.

Wild

Wild.

Our roots deeply planted as we sprout from the ground. We burst through the topsoil, searching for the light. Stretching our limbs out to the sun, asking that it meets us where we are.

We spot our brethren wildly growing and it encourages us to do the same. We reach a peak, entangle ourselves with one another and lean in.

Sometimes it feels like a brittle heaviness, other times the breeze hits us just right,
and we flow in the wind, freely.

We forge our path and allow others to traverse as they please, marking each footstep as a keystone of our worthiness, sometimes our loneliness too.

We'll keep growing wildly.

Giving wildly.

It's the only way of being.

Reflections: WildLife

WildFire:
Wildfire literally came to mind as my husband and I were driving through a wildfire. I felt like there was such a metaphor in the experience of us moving to a new state while paving new paths and navigating uncertainty. We were in the midst of ending an epic vacation out West and were driving to our new home in Colorado and everything felt heavy, new, uneasy, but also invigorating, all in the same breath. In hindsight, I knew things were getting ready to shift but I didn't have an idea of how much I'd need this poem over the course of the three years that followed during our time in Colorado.

Replenished Duality:
Replenished Duality was written as my husband and I were driving on curvy roads in Portugal. We stopped to orient ourselves in order to get to our destination and I noticed the brush, the weeds, and the nature around us. I found beauty in the resting nature, and the beauty in the flourishing one as well. It was a natural metaphor for how I wanted to live my life. More grateful for the balance. A life of knowing my buried season meant that eventually I'd bloom again; the ability to lean into rest in both seasons is absolutely necessary.

Wild:

Wild is similar to Replenished Duality. I was sitting in nature and admiring how things were flowing, how many of them were intertwined. I immediately thought about the roots in my life and how at times I needed sun, shade, and watering. But in other times, I needed to be the one providing those things to my village. We encourage one another to grow, shift and change, and that's what a rooted community should continuously do. I felt in this reflection that I was able to live wildly and encourage my tribe to leave just as freely but in their own timings.

Okay! I See You!

Protecting My Peace

My hand lay strategically placed on my sword:
the double-breasted gold plated one I've crafted
over the last three decades to survive, to protect
what always should've been mine, but one I
hadn't become fully acquainted with until my
mid-twenties.

A sword where the blade is laced with
boundaries. Where each groove determines how
many boundaries I'll have to erect, which is
typically dependent upon the person too.

I had to set aside those traditional beliefs that I
had to maintain peace at the sake of sacrificing
myself.
I've had to learn how not to lose track of the
melody in my heart. It's been the cadence of my
peace.

The added rigidity to my once-flexible sword
requires me to allow grace for the changes now,
remembering not to strip myself of the pleasure
and peace that can come with knowing other
humans, but also being willing to go to war for
myself because I won't be the sacrificial lamb any
longer.

A warrior's heart, my hand strategically placed
on my sword. The double-breasted gold plated
one I've crafted over the last three decades. To

protect what has always been mine, and what will always be mine.

Teetering Progression

Teetering back and forth on the uncharted belief that my dreams are worthy.

Hit the bottom too hard and my dreams floated into the air.

As if the bottom was made of clouds and the weight was unbearable.

Silently whispering, "You're not moving backward, you're just moving slow."

An unsteady balance as I tremble to my feet, fumbling through the thoughts in my mind.

"It's time to let go," I hear, as I reflect on those rising emotions.

Space

You can… You can…
You will… You will…
You already do….
Take up space.

A universal smile that breaks heart barriers just
by being who you are. An undeniable form of
energy that no one in your presence can deny.
Where my space is your space too… until you try
me. When the contents of my cosmic liveliness
leaves an everlasting impression.

You can…
You will…
You already do…
Take up space.

When your voice expands like lightning and
boasts a thunderous response. When you walk in
a room and feel like you don't belong…

Hold your space.
How tears fall from your cheeks when you can't
seem to find your breath… sit in your space.
When you feel small and insignificant.
Remember who you are and… hold your space.

You can…
You will…
You already do…
Take up space.

Silence Is Dangerous

There's a danger in silencing yourself.
No... not the "let me sit down, cross my legs,
meditation" silence... but the one where your
voice is not as boisterous as the melancholy
tempo beating in your chest.

The one where you press mute on your greatness
and suffer from not comprehending your own
worth. There is a risk in silencing yourself. The
silencing of my voice has served no purpose.

If I cannot sing a beautiful song to soothe a
broken heart, or speak up for those whose voices
have been silent for far longer than mine, then
what is the gift in having my voice box?

There is an insecurity in silencing yourself.
Where your thoughts retire to a grave of
unspoken beauty. And the world is stripped of
your delicacy. Like a glass shattering into
fragments, your voice is meant to make a sound.

The silencing of your voice will NEVER serve a
purpose.

Stretch Marks

My husband looks at me and says,
"You've always been comfortable in your body."

I shy away into a cocoon and ponder, partially
knowing his statement is true. But he doesn't
remember or, better yet, know the days when I
looked at the stretch marks slithering across my
body and wondered silently why I allowed myself
to expand and contract over and over again.

I sit in this thought a while longer…
Life is like that… an expansion of one's self into
spaces we'd never imagined possible, and a
retraction back to self for re-evaluation. And the
process starts all over again—if we allow it.

And I've allowed it, too.

A process of mental, physical and emotional
battles showing up as scarring on my skin, baring
a different color than the one I came here with,
perhaps. Where my periods of rapid growth
stretched me in more ways than I can count, and
the snap back of the long strides eased as I pulled
myself back into my own bosom to find comfort.
Marks etched all over my body, reminding me I
can shape shift and not be ashamed. That the
world may look upon them and not accept them.
That I'm still okay. That if I ever need to save

myself again, I have multiple reminders that I can and I will.

My husband looks at me and says, "You've always been comfortable in your body."

I respond, "I'm continually learning how to be."

Bare Soul

I've bared my soul in a hand cup, but I've never been naked. Stripped my face of masks full of pomp and circumstance. Torn down to the tattered masks that dangle from my skin that only I can see. Everything falling to the wayside yet the history of me still lingers. I'm working hard at it… because I've never truly been naked, just bare skinned really.

Today, I strip down and present myself with the battered bare pieces that I've hidden in the shadows. Present them scattered on a platter because presentation no longer matters here. Expose all the rough edges callously smoothed out, but only just a little. I come with all that I am, understanding that that is more than enough.

Pixie Dust

We are ALL made of pixie dust. A concoction of exponential memories sparked around the age of three.

Carving ourselves to fit into whatever environmental structures were in. We crave eventually being whole.

Constantly recapping the moments we've lived through. Suddenly, we're jolted out of construction and told to forgo the entire blueprint.

They yell, "Forget what we have done in the past! Look forward to the future and get this done instead." How easily they forget that even moving in a different direction required reviewing the previous and current construction designs.

Failing to grasp the concept of being in the present. Our perception of wholeness shifts.

Reflections: Okay! I See You!

"Okay! I see you!" is a common phrase in the Black collective. It is an acknowledgment that what one is doing is being recognized. It's a compliment, and when I see people grow, I love to encourage the continuation of that. This last section of the book reflects my growing pains over the last decade of my life; how I'm learning that my voice is powerful and that I am worthy of the spaces I embody.

Protecting My Peace:
Protecting My Peace was created from a prompt in a poetry environment I frequented during my time in Chicago. The challenge was to write something based on the topic of protecting my peace and though I wrote a ton that night, I thought this one was a reflection of my own personal journey of learning boundaries and enacting them. Healing isn't easy, but with practice and patience I am learning that the journey will not be linear, and that I can utilize what I'm learning to help catapult me into new stages in my life, that the tools I am gaining by growing are useful in many spaces.

Teetering Progression:
Teetering Progression was created while I was contemplating how I'd let my dreams kind of float into the air because life had knocked me down one too many times. I began to feel as

though I wasn't worthy enough to pursue my dreams and that none of them would come to fruition, that my failures outweighed my ability to move forward.

Space:
Space is a poem that encourages me—and others—to take up each and every space that we find ourselves in, to know and believe that we are worthy enough to take up space. I'm learning to do this even when my voice shakes, even when I've let the perceived perception reel roll through my mind prior to entering the space, and I'm learning how to cope with my own anxieties of taking up space.

Silence Is Dangerous:
I wrote this poem during a time in my life where I had been let go from my job and I had to learn to fight for myself in order to not be unfairly treated. In writing this poem, I realized that being silent was prevalent in my life, and that I had a learned behavior of staying silent instead of asking for what I needed or standing up for myself.

Stretch Marks:
I was turning twenty-nine and I was obsessed with looking at my body. At this point in my life the biggest I had been (well, at least documented) was two-hundred-twenty-seven pounds. I have stretch marks on my arms, legs

and back, and I was learning how to be okay with their presence on my body. This poem was necessary for me to release, because I began to understand that prior to this moment I hadn't really focused on what my body looked like from the perception of what the world thought I should be. It allowed me to take some power back and lay to rest the societal burdens that lie on women's bodies.

Bare Soul:
As I'm continually growing, I realized that I'd have to remove the masks I had picked up in order to protect myself. I wanted to strip down to the most authentic me. I wanted to show up as the most authentic me that I could be in every moment. That didn't just mean the happy moments, but also all the emotions that we try to avoid: sadness, fear, doubt, and everything in between. I'm learning every day that showing up as my authentic self will always be enough.

Pixie Dust:
As I am challenging the ideas of perception and their importance in my life, Pixie Dust represents how I don't want to continue carving myself for the likes of someone else. That my perspectives and others' perspectives placed upon me can be challenged and these should not be entangled with my worthiness.

Reflection

Utilize this section to reflect on your own life's experiences. This can include parental relationships, romantic relationships, or the relationship you have with yourself. Keep in mind that the reflection is not limited to just those things. Let your mind flow and make some space for yourself to reflect.

Made in the USA
Coppell, TX
09 September 2022